Destination Detectives

Egypt

North America

Europe

EGYPT

Asia

Africa

South America

Australasia

Nicola Barber

www.raintreepublishers.co.uk
Visit our website to find out more information about **Raintree** books.

To order:
☎ Phone 44 (0) 1865 888112
🖹 Send a fax to 44 (0) 1865 314091
💻 Visit the Raintree Bookshop at **www.raintreepublishers.co.uk** to browse our catalogue and order online.

Produced for Raintree by
White-Thomson Publishing Ltd,
Bridgewater Business Centre,
210 High Street, Lewes, BN7 2NH

First published in Great Britain by Raintree,
Halley Court, Jordan Hill, Oxford OX2 8EJ,
Part of Harcourt Education.
Raintree is a registered trademark of
Harcourt Education Ltd.

© Harcourt Education Ltd 2006
The moral right of the proprietor has been asserted.

Editorial: Sonya Newland, Melanie Waldron,
and Lucy Beevor
Design: Clare Nicholas
Picture Research: Amy Sparks
Production: Chloe Bloom

Originated by Modern Age
Printed and bound in China
by South China Printing Company

10 digit ISBN 1406203106
13 digit ISBN 9781406203103
10 9 8 7 6 5 4 3 2 1
11 10 09 08 07 06

British Library Cataloguing in Publication Data
Barber, Nicola
    Egypt. - (Destination detectives)
    1.Egypt - Geography - Juvenile literature 2.Egypt - Social
life and customs - 21st century - Juvenile literature
    3.Egypt - Civilization - Juvenile literature
    I.Title
    962'.055

Acknowledgements
The Art Archive pp. 19; Corbis pp. 10, 12 (Rob Howard),
16 (Tibor Bognár), 18-19 (Patrick Durand), 20-21 (Ron
Watts), 21 (Hans Georg Roth), 29b (Attar Maher),
31 (Richard T. Nowitz), 33 (Sandro Vannini), 32-33,
34-35, 38 (Arthur Thévenart); Ecoscene pp. 6b (Reinhard
Dirscherl), 42 (Reinhard Dirscherl); Getty Images
pp. 43 (Robert Harding World Imagery); iStockphoto
pp. 40-41; Photolibrary pp. 4-3 (Jon Arnold Images),
8 (Robert Harding Picture Library), 11 (Jon Arnold Images),
13 (Jon Arnold Images), 14-15 (Index Stock Imagery),
15 (Index Stock Imagery), 24 (Chris Mclennan
Photography), 35t (Robert Harding Picture Library);
Popperfoto pp. 36-37; Topfoto pp. 9 (HIP/Ann Ronan
Picture Library), 25 (Werner Forman Archive), 28 (IMW),
39 (Dr Elmar R. Gruber), 41 (Hubertus Kanus); WTPix
pp. 5t, 5m, 5b, 6t, 17, 18, 22, 23, 26, 27, 29t, 30, 36, 40.

Cover photograph of Great Pyramids at Giza reproduced
with permission of Photolibrary/Jon Arnold Images.

Every effort has been made to contact copyright
holders of any material reproduced in this book.
Any omissions will be rectified in subsequent
printings if notice is given to the publishers.

Disclaimer
All the Internet addresses (URLs) given in this book were
valid at the time of going to press. However, due to the
dynamic nature of the Internet, some addresses may have
changed or ceased to exist since publication. While the
author and publishers regret any inconvenience this may
cause readers, no responsibility for any such changes can be
accepted by either the author or the publishers.

Contents

Any words appearing in the text in bold, **like this,** are explained in the glossary. You can also look out for them in the Word Bank box at the bottom of each page.

Where in the world?

Beneath the desert sands

The temple of Pharaoh Ramses II was carved out of the rock over 3,000 years ago. As the centuries passed, the desert sands gradually covered the temple. It was rediscovered in 1813 by a Swiss explorer, Jean-Louis Burckhardt, who noticed a huge head sticking out of the sand.

You awake to the sound of lapping water and a gentle rocking motion. Although it is early, already it's hot, and through your **porthole** you can see that the sky is a deep, cloudless blue. As you take a look outside, the most amazing sight greets your startled eyes!

Four huge stone figures sit, hands on knees. One of the figures has lost its head, the other three stare at you and beyond you, as they have done for centuries. The stone figures look as if they are guarding something – but what?

The massive statues of Ramses II guard the Great Temple at Abu Simbel.

WORD BANK   pharaoh king or queen in ancient Egyptian times

You run ashore along one of the jetties connecting your boat to the edge of the lake. Close up, the stone figures look even more impressive – they must be at least 18 metres (60 feet) high. A sign catches your eye: "Great Temple of Ramses II". You know from your history classes that Ramses was one of the Egyptian **pharaohs**. You must be in Egypt!

In fact, the four massive statues are all Ramses II, and this was his temple. Ramses was one of the long line of pharaohs who ruled ancient Egypt between 5,000 and 2,000 years ago. It's time to find out more about them, and about life in modern-day Egypt.

Find out later...

Where is the world's longest river?

What sound will you hear coming from these towers?

How do Egyptian children spend their free time?

All about Egypt

Egypt at a glance

POPULATION:
77.5 million

CAPITAL:
Cairo

AREA:
1,001,450 square kilometres
(386,660 square miles)

RELIGION:
Islam

OFFICIAL LANGUAGE:
Arabic

CURRENCY:
Egyptian pound (E£)

GOVERNMENT:
Republic

Back in your cabin, you notice that someone has left behind a map of Egypt. You open it up to find a big red ring drawn around Abu Simbel, on the shores of Lake Nasser. So that's where you are! Abu Simbel lies in the far south of Egypt, only 40 kilometres (25 miles) from the border with Sudan. Looking at the map, you can see that there is a huge amount of Egypt to explore to the north, the north-west, and the north-east.

Cairo is the capital of Egypt. It is a mixture of ancient and new, and is one of the most crowded cities in the world.

Tourists come from all over the world to see the spectacular underwater life of Egypt's Red Sea coast.

North of Cairo, the River Nile splits into many different channels before it flows out into the Mediterranean Sea. This area is known as the Nile **Delta**.

WORD BANK   delta area where a river splits into several channels as it flows into the sea

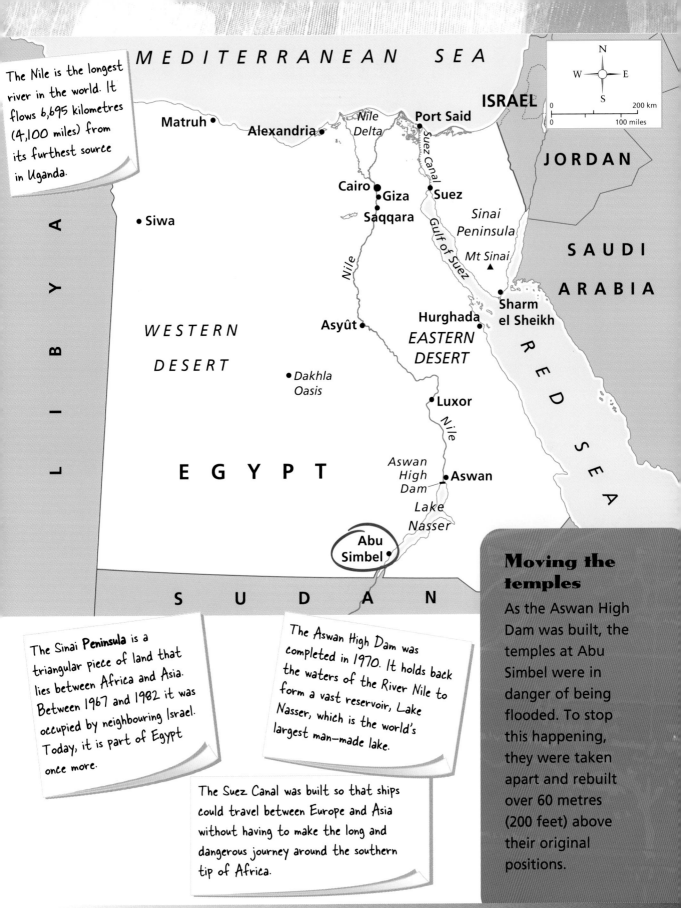

MEDITERRANEAN SEA

The Nile is the longest river in the world. It flows 6,695 kilometres (4,100 miles) from its furthest source in Uganda.

Matruh

Alexandria

Nile Delta

Port Said

ISRAEL

JORDAN

Suez Canal

Cairo

Giza

Suez

Saqqara

Siwa

Sinai Peninsula

Mt Sinai

Gulf of Suez

SAUDI

ARABIA

WESTERN DESERT

Nile

Asyût

Hurghada

Sharm el Sheikh

EASTERN DESERT

Dakhla Oasis

RED SEA

Luxor

EGYPT

Nile

Aswan High Dam

Aswan

Lake Nasser

Abu Simbel

SUDAN

Moving the temples

As the Aswan High Dam was built, the temples at Abu Simbel were in danger of being flooded. To stop this happening, they were taken apart and rebuilt over 60 metres (200 feet) above their original positions.

The Sinai **Peninsula** is a triangular piece of land that lies between Africa and Asia. Between 1967 and 1982 it was occupied by neighbouring Israel. Today, it is part of Egypt once more.

The Aswan High Dam was completed in 1970. It holds back the waters of the River Nile to form a vast reservoir, Lake Nasser, which is the world's largest man-made lake.

The Suez Canal was built so that ships could travel between Europe and Asia without having to make the long and dangerous journey around the southern tip of Africa.

peninsula narrow area of land that sticks out into the sea or a lake

Ancient Egypt

Ramses II was just one of a long line of **pharaohs** who ruled Egypt from about 3100 BC to 30 BC, when Egypt became part of the Roman Empire. The first pharaoh was Narmer (also called Menes), who united the settlements along the Nile River to make a single state. The ancient Egyptians invented the world's earliest writing – a type of picture writing called **hieroglyphics**. They worshipped many different gods and goddesses, and built huge temples throughout their kingdom.

The Sun God

One of the most important of all the ancient Egyptian gods and goddesses was the Sun God. Although the Sun God had several different names, the most common was Ra. Ra was often shown in wall paintings and carvings as a man with a **falcon**'s head, with a circular sun on top.

The pyramids

People come from all over the world to marvel at the temples and other monuments that survive from ancient Egyptian times. The most awe-inspiring of these are the pyramids. The first of these huge, four-sided structures was built by Pharaoh Djoser (Zoser) in about 2650 BC. Around 60 years later, Pharaoh Khufu built the biggest of all the pyramids, the Great Pyramid at Giza.

The Great Pyramid at Giza was one of the Seven Wonders of the Ancient ► World.

Great Pyramid facts

- Made from over 2 million blocks of stone.
- Some of the blocks weigh as much as 15 tonnes (16.5 tons).
- The four sides are 230 metres (756 feet) long.
- Over 100,000 workers built the Pyramid.
- It took more than 20 years to build.
- It is 140 metres (482 feet) high.

WORD BANK   afterlife life after death
falcon bird of prey, often used for hunting

What were they for?

The pyramids were burial places for the pharaohs. The body of the pharaoh was placed under or inside the pyramid. The ancient Egyptians believed in life after death, so the pharaoh was buried with everything necessary for the **afterlife** – food, furniture, clothes, and treasures.

Mummies

In ancient Egypt, the bodies of pharaohs and other important people were preserved after death. This is called mummification. First, special priests removed all the organs from the body except the heart. Then they dried the body out, wrapped it in linen, and placed it in a painted coffin.

The mummy of this ancient Egyptian princess lies inside a beautifully painted coffin.

◀

hieroglyphics type of writing that uses pictures

Landscape & climate

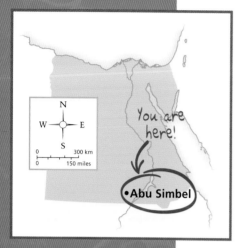

You are here!

•Abu Simbel

The easiest way to head north from Abu Simbel is down the Nile River, so you jump on board a *felucca*, a traditional boat with triangular sails. It is a very peaceful way to travel, and it gives you time to find out more about this amazing river. The Nile flows 1,600 kilometres (994 miles) from the southern border of Egypt northwards to its **delta** on the Mediterranean Sea. For thousands of years, the Nile's regular floods spread **fertile silt** across the land in its **floodplain**, allowing Egyptian farmers to grow their crops along each side of the river.

Dam benefits

Controlling the floods has made life much easier for people living along the Nile River. The huge amount of water trapped by the Aswan High Dam in Lake Nasser is used for **irrigating** fields and for year-round water supplies. Massive turbines in the dam generate **hydroelectric** power, supplying nearly a quarter of Egypt's electricity.

A traditional Egyptian *felucca* sails down the Nile River.

10   **WORD BANK**   floodplain area that floods when river water rises
hydroelectric energy created by moving water

Stopping the floods

In certain years the Nile has not flooded. This has resulted in drought and famine. At other times, the floods were so great that they washed away all the crops. To control the flooding, a dam was built across the Nile. The first dam was completed in 1902. At the time it was the largest dam in the world, but it was still not big enough to control the river.

The huge Aswan High Dam was built between 1960 and 1970, 6 kilometres (4 miles) upstream from the old dam. It finally put an end to the Nile's floods.

The Aswan High Dam controls the flooding of the Nile. Now that their fields are no longer fertilized by the rich silt, Egyptian farmers have to use more artificial fertilizers.

Lake Nasser

Lake Nasser is a vast expanse of blue in the middle of the desert. However, some people think that this huge lake could slowly disappear! Most of the silt that the Nile River used to wash towards its delta is now trapped by the Aswan High Dam, and this silt is gradually filling up the reservoir.

Fast fact

The Aswan High Dam is 111 metres (364 feet) high, and 3,830 metres (12,562 feet) long.

irrigating using water from a river or reservoir to grow crops in fields
silt mud and sand

Camels

The camel has been part of life in Egypt for thousands of years. It has been used for transport, for its meat and milk, and for wool and leather. The one-humped Arabian camel is well-suited to life in the desert. Its broad, padded feet support its weight on loose sand, and its eyes are protected by long eyelashes against blowing sand.

Desert regions

About 94 percent of Egypt's land surface is desert. To the west of the Nile River lies the vast Western Desert (also known as the Libyan Desert), which is part of the **Sahara**. Between the Red Sea and the east side of the Nile is the Eastern Desert. Across the Gulf of Suez, much of the Sinai **Peninsula** is also desert.

The Western Desert is a land of huge sand dunes, blown and shaped by the fierce desert winds. The Eastern Desert and the Sinai Peninsula are more rocky, with bare mountains and deep, dry river beds called **wadis**. The highest point in Egypt, Mount Katherine (2,537 metres/8,652 feet), is in the south of the Sinai Peninsula.

In Egypt's Western Desert, strong winds have created strange formations from rock and sand. ▼

Fast fact

A camel can survive for up to a week on just the fat stored in its hump.

12   **WORD BANK**   coral skeletons of tiny sea animals
Sahara largest desert in the world, covering much of North Africa

Coastlines

Egypt has coastlines along the Mediterranean Sea, the Red Sea, and around the Sinai Peninsula. Where the Nile flows into the Mediterranean it has formed a huge, fan-shaped **delta**, which is nearly 250 kilometres (155 miles) wide, along the coast. The Red Sea coast is famous for its beautiful turquoise waters and the amazing **coral** reefs that lie beneath the surface. There are also coral reefs off the coast of Sinai, and both regions attract thousands of tourists every year.

Sharm el-Sheikh, on the Sinai coast, is one of Egypt's most popular tourist destinations.

The Red Sea

The Red Sea is the only tropical sea in the world that is almost completely closed. No river flows into it, and only a small amount of water from the Indian Ocean flows through at its southern end.

wadi dried-up river bed

Climate

The weather in Egypt is much the same all year round – hot and dry! There are two main seasons. Temperatures in the summer season, from May to October, are scorchingly hot. The temperature in July reaches a high of 48.5°C (120°F) in the Western Desert, and 35°C (95°F) in Cairo. During the cooler season, from November to April, the average maximum temperature in Cairo and the desert is around 20°C (68°F). At night, it can be cold in the desert, with temperatures as low as 5°C (41°F).

The *khamsin*

During April and May, a wind known as the *khamsin* often blows from the **Sahara**. This hot, dry wind picks up dust and sand, turning the sky orange, and covering everything in its path with fine grit. The name *khamsin* comes from the Arabic word for "50", because this wind is said to blow for about 50 days every year.

The Sinai **Peninsula**, in north-eastern Egypt, has a dry, rocky landscape, with little or no rainfall.

Fast fact

Alexandria has more rain than anywhere else in Egypt – up to 18 cm (7 inches) a year. Cairo has an average of just 2.2 cm (0.9 inches), while most of Egypt has no rainfall at all.

No need to pack an umbrella!

Egypt has virtually no rain, except along the northern coast during the cooler season. Alexandria has on average five days of rain in January, and three days of rain in February, November, and December. For the rest of the year there is practically no rain at all. In Aswan, the average rainfall throughout the whole year is zero!

▲ The Nubian ibex, a type of wild goat, lives in the dry desert regions of north-eastern Egypt.

Desert miracle

Every few years, rain falls on the parched, rocky landscape of the Sinai Peninsula. The **wadis** (dry river beds) fill with torrents of brown water, as **flash floods** roar through the hills. The rain brings to life seeds that have lain in the sand, and soon the land is covered in green shoots and flowers.

Getting around

Service taxis

Service taxis are big cars or minibuses that leave only when they are full. Drivers wait near bus and train stations and shout out a name to tell people where they are going. Service taxis are usually cheaper than buses and trains.

You are tempted to sail all the way down the Nile River, straight to Cairo, 1,000 kilometres (621 miles) away. However, you also want to explore the vast desert to the west of the river, so you say goodbye to the Nile and jump on a bus that will take you deep into the desert.

Buses and trains

Your bus is air-conditioned, which is a relief because it's hot outside! Long-distance buses link most of the cities, towns, and villages in Egypt. Some of them are comfortable, others are more basic, and they can get extremely crowded. An alternative is to take the train.

Cairo is one of the busiest cities in the world, and traffic jams are common.

WORD BANK   rural relating to the countryside

Train lines connect Egypt's major cities, and some of the trains have carriages with bunks. This means that passengers can sleep while the train carries them towards their destination through the night.

Cars and taxis

Driving in Egypt can be a bit chaotic. In Cairo, there are traffic jams almost all the time, as more than a million cars try to drive around the city every day. In **rural** areas, the roads are often quite rough, and potholes and drifts of sand make driving difficult. Many people use taxis to get around cities. In Cairo the taxis are black and white. In Alexandria they are black and orange.

River life

Up and down the length of the Nile, the river is used for transport. For tourists visiting Egypt, travelling on the river is a fantastic way to see the country. Many luxury cruise boats, as well as *feluccas*, sail along the river, particularly between Luxor and Aswan.

Pleasure boats, like these at Luxor, take tourists on trips up and down the Nile River.

Metro and trams

Cairo has the only **metro** system in Egypt – in fact, in the whole of Africa. The metro has two lines, although a third is being built and more lines are planned for the future. Alexandria has no metro, but it does have a **tram** system. On both the metro and the tram, some carriages are for women only, so that women can sit separately from male passengers if they want to.

Air travel

Egypt's main cities and tourist centres all have international airports. There are also many smaller airports for flights within the country.

People crowd on to a bus in Cairo.

Watch where you go!

Driving off the roads can be dangerous in some parts of Egypt. Near El-Alamein, just west of Alexandria on the Mediterranean coast, there are land mines left from World War II. Around the Suez Canal, mines from the **Arab-Israeli wars** still lurk in the sands.

WORD BANK Arab-Israeli wars several wars fought between Israel and the Arab states in the 20th century

These include places such as Aswan and Abu Simbel in the south, St Katherine's in the Sinai **Peninsula**, and the Kharga and Siwa **oases** in the Western Desert.

The Suez Canal

The Suez Canal stretches 163 kilometres (101 miles) from Port Said on the Mediterranean Sea to Suez at the northern end of the Gulf of Suez. It allows ships to travel from the Mediterranean through to the Red Sea, and from there into the Indian Ocean. It is the fastest sea route from Europe to Asia. The canal is about 1 kilometre (0.6 miles) wide. It is very busy, and up to 25,000 ships use it every year.

The Suez Canal has just one lane for ships, with passing places along the way. ▶

Canal history

It took nearly eleven years to build the Suez Canal. Thousands of Egyptian labourers dug most of it by hand, and hundreds died each year as a result of the terrible conditions in which they worked. When the canal finally opened in 1869, there were great celebrations, with fireworks and a grand ball for 6,000 people.

The first ships sail down the Suez Canal in 1869. ▼

Desert regions

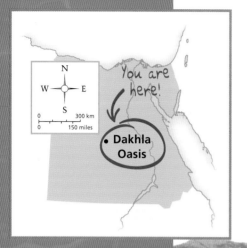

You are here!

Dakhla Oasis

After five or so hours on the bus, you arrive at your desert destination, Dakhla **Oasis**. After the rocky, sandy desert landscape, it's a shock to drive through the lush, green fields of the oasis. So much seems to grow here! You can see palm trees loaded with dates, orange, apricot, and olive trees, as well as fields of wheat and rice. It is amazing to find all this in the middle of the desert!

What is an oasis?

Deep underneath the desert, there is water. In some places in the Western Desert, the land dips down so low that the water lies near the surface. The result is an oasis, that is, an area where freshwater springs provide enough water for people to live and to grow their crops.

The village of Al-Qasr in the Dakhla Oasis, showing the lush green trees of the oasis against the desert landscape.

Sand dunes

The crescent-shaped dunes that lie across the great Western Desert have a special name – barchans.

WORD BANK   fertile land that is good for growing crops
oasis fertile area in the middle of a desert

In fact, Dakhla is not the only oasis in the Western Desert. There are four others – Kharga, Farafra, and Bahariyya, and in the far north-west of the desert, Siwa. These oases are like small, **fertile** islands surrounded by the vast desert sands.

The Great Sand Sea

The Western Desert covers about two-thirds of the land surface of Egypt. The Great Sand Sea extends 72,000 square kilometres (28,000 square miles) across much of the Western Desert and into Libya. This huge area of sand is one of the largest in the world. It is made up of huge dunes that are constantly changing shape and position as they are blown by the wind.

A man collects water in the Dakhla Oasis.

Prehistoric paintings

We know from ancient paintings found on rocks that people have lived in the Dakhla Oasis since **prehistoric** times. There was once a huge lake in this area, and the paintings show elephants, buffaloes, and ostriches on its shores.

Desert people

Most of the people who live in Egypt can trace their **ancestors** back to the ancient Egyptians and the **Muslim Arabs** who invaded the country in the 7th century. However, Egypt's deserts are also home to some people from different **ethnic groups**.

In the Western Desert around Siwa, the Berbers have their own way of life and language. The Berbers are descended from the people who lived in North Africa before the arrival of the Muslim Arabs. In Siwa, Berbers speak their own version of the Berber language, called Siwi. Berber women in Siwa wear beautiful silver jewellery, and are famous for their skill at weaving baskets from the leaves of palm trees.

The Bedouin

The name Bedouin comes from an Arabic word meaning "people of the desert". The Bedouin are Arabs who long ago learned how to live in the harsh desert with their camels and herds of goats and sheep.

Bedouin costume

Bedouin men usually wear long white tunics. They also wear a headdress, tied with a black headband called a *kaffia*. Bedouin women wear black, and cover their heads and faces with a veil called a *bourque*. They also like to wear jewellery, some of which can be worth a lot of money.

A Bedouin family in the Sinai **Peninsula**. The man wears the traditional white tunic and headdress.

WORD BANK   ancestor person you are descended from
Arab person who originally came from the Arabian Peninsula

Traditionally, the Bedouin moved from place to place, taking their camel-hair tents with them, to find grazing for their animals. About 50,000 Bedouin still live in the Sinai Peninsula, but today many have settled in one place.

The Nubians

The dark-skinned Nubians come from the area between Aswan in southern Egypt and Khartoum in Sudan. Their culture started at about the same time as that of the ancient Egyptians, 5,000 years ago.

A Nubian man uses traditional mud bricks for building in a village on Elephantine Island in the Nile.

ethnic group people who share customs, beliefs, and often language
henna natural plant dye

Egypt's cities

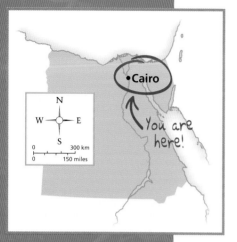

Cairo

You are here!

From the peace and beauty of the desert, you have arrived in busy, chaotic Cairo. After your long bus journey, you need to find somewhere to relax and have a drink. Where better than one of the city's many coffee houses? You decide to visit one of the oldest and most famous of them all: Fishawi's, in the Khan al-Khalili **bazaar**. It's open every day, all day and all night – and you will be able to buy delicious, refreshing *chai* (mint tea). You can sit, watch the world go by, and decide what to do next in Cairo.

The Nilometer

At the southern tip of Rhoda Island in Cairo is a Nilometer. The ancient Egyptians built several of these devices to measure the amount of water in the Nile, and to predict whether or not the river would flood. If the water level was high then the harvest was likely to be good. If it was low, there were anxious times ahead.

People have been trading at the Khan al-Khalili bazaar since the **Middle Ages**.

Survival tip
There are usually no fixed prices at Egyptian bazaars, so you can haggle with the stall-holder about the cost of an item.

WORD BANK bazaar covered market full of stalls and small shops
Middle Ages period of history from the 5th to the 15th centuries

Cairo choices

Cairo is huge, and it's difficult to know where to start, so you make a list:

- Khan al-Khalili – you are already sitting in this bustling bazaar because that's where Fishawi's is found. You decide to explore the narrow alleyways full of shops and stalls before moving on to…
- Mosque of al-Azhar – this **mosque** was founded in AD 970, and quickly became a centre of learning in the **Muslim** world. Today, it is said to be the oldest university in the world.
- Egyptian Museum – this contains more than 140,000 items from ancient Egypt, including the contents of the tomb of the boy-**pharaoh**, Tutankhamun.
- The Nile – join the crowds for an evening walk along the Corniche el-Nil, the winding road that follows the course of the river.

The magnificent death-mask of Pharaoh Tutankhamun. ➤

Tutankhamun

The boy-pharaoh Tutankhamun ruled Egypt from around 1336–1327 BC. He is famous today because of the discovery of his tomb in 1922. The tomb was hidden in the Valley of the Kings, and it was stuffed full of amazing treasures, including a death-mask made from solid gold, and Tutankhamun's clothes.

mosque place of worship for Muslims

The City of the Dead

For some poor people in Cairo, a tomb is their home. The City of the Dead is a network of large cemeteries that lie at the base of the Muqattam Hills to the east of the city. Many of the grand tombs in the cemeteries are like small houses, and thousands of Egyptians live there.

Life in the city

Cairo is one of the most overcrowded cities in the world. Between 1970 and 2000 its population doubled from five to ten million, as huge numbers of people moved from the countryside to start new lives in the city.

The arrival of so many people has caused major problems with housing. Many families live in very cramped conditions, squashed into one-room flats. Often there is no running water. Thousands of people are so poor that they live and work around the city's main rubbish dump, sorting the rubbish to make a living.

People huddle in a makeshift shelter. These often serve as homes in the poorer parts of Cairo.
➤

WORD BANK cemetery place where dead people are buried in graves or tombs

Breathing the air

Air pollution is another big problem in Cairo. Much of the pollution comes from the cars and other vehicles that clog the city's streets every day. The Egyptian Government is tackling the problem by trying to persuade drivers to convert their vehicles to **compressed natural gas** (CNG). This fuel is much cleaner and cheaper than diesel or petrol.

Education

Egypt's universities are highly regarded in the **Arab** world, particularly the university at Cairo. However, many Egyptian adults, especially women, cannot either read or write. Children start school when they are six, and by law must spend six years at primary school and three years at intermediate school. In some places, though, especially in the countryside, many children do not go to school at all, especially after the age of eleven.

Fast fact

Percentage of Egyptians over the age of 15 who can read and write:
Total population:
57.7 percent
Male:
68.3 percent
Female:
46.9 percent

What's the news?

There are many daily newspapers in Egypt. The most popular is *Al-Akbar*. In a country where so many people cannot read or write, television is also very important, with lots of channels to choose from.

Literacy levels for women in Egypt are quite low, as many girls leave school earlier than boys.

compressed natural gas gas from beneath the ground that has been squeezed into a container and can be used as a fuel

The call to prayer

After a good night's sleep you awake to the sound of a *muezzin* giving the call to prayer from a nearby **minaret**. **Muslims** must pray five times every day. Muslim men can go to the **mosque** to pray, or they can simply stop what they are doing to pray at home, on the street, or at work. Muslim women usually pray at home.

Islam

The people of Egypt are mostly followers of the religion of Islam, known as Muslims. Islam is based on the teachings of the Prophet Muhammad, who was born in Makkah, in present-day Saudi Arabia. The Prophet Muhammad died in AD 632, and within ten years the new religion of Islam had arrived in Egypt, as Muslim armies swept into the country and took control.

The Copts

A visit to the Hanging Church in Cairo reminds you that before the arrival of Islam, Christianity was the main religion in Egypt. The Egyptian Coptic Church is a separate branch of Christianity, with its own leader. Today, services are still held in the ancient Coptic language.

Religion in Egypt
*Muslim: 94 percent
Coptic Christian and others:
6 percent.*

Monks celebrating morning mass ➤ at a Coptic monastery.

WORD BANK minaret tall tower, usually built as part of a mosque

Islam means "submission" or "obedience" to Allah – the Arabic word for God. Muslims often think of their religion as a strong building held up by five pillars. These "five pillars" help Muslims to lead good lives. They are:

The Mohammad Ali mosque in Cairo. The call to prayer is given from the tall towers, called minarets. ▶

- Belief: The most important belief of Islam is stated in the shahadah – "There is no God except Allah, Muhammad is the messenger of Allah."
- Prayer: Muslims pray five times every day, facing Makkah.
- Alms: Muslims must give money to charity.
- Fasting: Every year, during the month of Ramadan, Muslims fast during the hours of daylight.
- Pilgrimage: Every Muslim who can, must make a pilgrimage to Makkah once in his or her lifetime. This is called the *hajj*.

Moulid an-Nabi

Egyptians celebrate the birth of the Prophet Muhammad every year at the festival of Moulid an-Nabi. There are colourful street parades with lights and drummers, and special sweets for the children!

Muslim men gather for prayer outside the Al-Azhar mosque in Cairo. ▼

Luxor

Luxor lies on the Nile River, on the site of the capital of ancient Egypt, Thebes. The modern Egyptian town stands next to countless ancient monuments, and it is a major tourist centre. People come here to visit the magnificent temple complex.

The mega-city

What other cities could you visit in Egypt? You look at your map. Alexandria, on the Mediterranean coast, is Egypt's second city. The rest of Egypt's large cities are all in the Nile **Delta**, which is where the majority of Egyptians live. Places such as Al-Giza and Shubra Al-Khaymah are part of the vast sprawl of Greater Cairo, known as a **"mega-city"**.

Alexandria

Alexandria is named after its founder, the ancient Greek general Alexander the Great, who started the construction of the city in 332 BC. Alexandria became a grand and wealthy city, famous for its academics, and a rival to ancient Rome. One of the Seven Wonders of the Ancient World, the Pharos (lighthouse), stood in its harbour. Today, the city is Egypt's main port. It is also a tourist centre, particularly for people from Cairo, who head to Egypt's north coast to escape the summer heat.

The temple complex at Luxor attracts thousands of visitors to the area every year.

WORD BANK   mega-city huge urban area, often including several cities

Other places to visit

Port Said lies on the Mediterranean Sea, at the northern end of the Suez Canal. It was founded in 1859 as a base for the workers who were digging the canal.

Suez lies on the Gulf of Suez at the southern end of the Suez Canal. It has been a port for many centuries. Like Port Said, it was bombed and badly damaged during the wars with Israel in 1967 and 1973.

Asyut stands on a crossroads between the River Nile and trade routes to the Western Desert **oases** and beyond. It has long been a centre of trade, and once had the biggest slave market in Egypt.

Aswan is Egypt's most southerly city. The city was an important trading centre, and today is very popular with tourists, particularly during the cooler months.

An ancient centre of learning

Alexandria was home to one of the most famous libraries of the ancient world. Sadly, the library and many of its books were destroyed in the 5th century, but a new library has just been built in the city to house rare and ancient manuscripts and books.

Fishing boats in the harbour of the ancient city of Alexandria.

Food & farming

Hummus

Egyptians love to eat this delicious dip:

1 can (425g) chickpeas

1/3 cup **tahini**

1/4 cup lemon juice

3/4 cup olive oil

3 cloves crushed garlic

salt and black pepper to taste

Mash the chickpeas and mix with the other ingredients. Serve with warm pitta bread.

While exploring Cairo, you have discovered the joys of the roadside juice bars. Here, you can get fresh and refreshing drinks made from squeezing whatever fruit happens to be in season – bananas, lemons, mangoes, strawberries, and pomegranates to name but a few. Now it's time for something to eat.

You find a street stall that is selling *aish* – flat, pitta-like bread, stuffed with *fuul*. This typical Egyptian food is made from small, brown **fava beans**, which are soaked, boiled, and mashed, then mixed with lemon juice, herbs, and oil. Next to it is another stall selling a popular fast food called *ta'amiyya* – mashed fava beans that have been deep-fried. Further down the street, another favourite national dish is on offer, *kushari*. This is a delicious mixture of pasta, rice, lentils, and tomato sauce, topped with spicy fried onions.

This street stall displays baskets containing many different types of Egyptian spices.

WORD BANK   fava bean small bean that grows in pods

Ramadan

Ramadan is the ninth month in the Islamic calendar. During this month, **Muslims** do not eat or drink during the hours of daylight (see page 29). When the call to prayer rings out at sunset, people eat a meal called *iftar*. Families eat together, and the restaurants in Cairo and other cities are packed through the night. Just before sunrise, people eat their second meal of the night, called *sohour*, before the daytime fast starts again.

A man cooks *fatir* – Egyptian pancakes.

Sweet treats

Ramadan may be a time of fasting, but during the hours of darkness, people traditionally eat special sweet pastries. These include *kunafa*, a type of shredded wheat with raisins, nuts, and cream. Another favourite is *qatayef* – a pastry stuffed with pistachios, almonds, and raisins, and covered with a sugary lemon syrup.

tahini paste made from sesame seeds

Growing food

In the countryside, many Egyptians grow the food that they and their families eat. Farmers have been tending their crops in the Nile Valley and **Delta** for thousands of years. They have always relied on water from the river, as there is not enough rainfall in Egypt for crops to grow.

Today, a third of Egypt's population still works on the land. Some of these people work on large, **mechanized** farms growing crops for export such as cotton. But most are peasant farmers, called *fellahin*. The *fellahin* own or rent small plots of land to grow crops such as wheat, barley, maize, and vegetables to feed their families. If they can, they also grow **cash crops**, such as dates or sugar cane, which they can take to the local market to sell. Many *fellahin* have donkeys to carry loads, and a goat for milk.

The first farmers
The ancient Egyptians were the first people to grow cereal crops, such as wheat and barley, about 7,000 years ago.

WORD BANK cash crop crop that is grown for the farmer to sell

Irrigation

Very little would grow in Egypt's dry soils if it were not for **irrigation**. The ancient Egyptians were experts at storing, moving, and distributing water from the Nile River. They invented the *shaduf*, a long pole with a bucket on one end to scoop up water, and the water wheel, which is usually driven by a cow or an ox. Both these methods of lifting and moving water are still used in **rural** areas of Egypt today.

Water wheels, or *sakiya*, are driven by animals.

A farm worker tills the land with a cattle-drawn plough near Cairo.

Ancient Egyptian treats

We know from paintings that the ancient Egyptians ate extremely well. The **fertile** Nile Valley provided them with cereals, fruits, and vegetables, as well as fish from the river, and birds such as ducks and geese.

Sport & culture

It's time for some fun! There is a soccer match at the Cairo Stadium between the city's two big clubs, Al-Ahly and Zamalek. The stadium is huge – it can hold 100,000 people – and it's packed for this important match between two old rivals in the National League.

Café life

Egyptians go to coffee houses, called *ahwa*, to meet their friends, read the newspapers, watch football on television, and play backgammon and dominoes. Mostly it is men who spend time in the coffee houses, but in the big cities it is becoming more common to see mixed groups of men and women enjoying café life together.

Favourite sports

Although most Egyptians are soccer-mad, other sports are popular too. The long-distance swimmer Abdellatief Abouheif is a national hero who achieved many swimming records during the 1950s and 1960s. Squash is also popular, and every year there is an international squash tournament.

Students play soccer in a school playground in Giza – soccer is the most popular sport in Egypt.

The squash games are played in a special glass court set up next to the pyramids at Giza. Another sport that makes use of Egypt's ancient history is running. The Pharaonic Race is 100 kilometres (62 miles), and is based on an ancient Egyptian race, which tested the fitness of the **Pharaoh**'s soldiers. The race starts in the **oasis** of al-Fayoum, south-west of Cairo, and ends at the pyramids of Saqqara.

Let's see a movie

A trip to the cinema is always fun in Egypt. You can see a locally produced film in Arabic, or the latest Hollywood hit. There's lots of cheering or booing, depending what's happening on the screen!

The "Star of the East"

Music can be heard everywhere in Egypt, from Western pop to street musicians playing traditional instruments. The biggest star in Egyptian music was the singer Umm Kulthum. Once a month, the whole country came to a standstill as Umm Kulthum broadcast a live performance on national radio.

Egypt (in red and white) takes on Senegal in the huge stadium at Cairo during a World Cup qualifier.

Dancing Egypt-style

We know from paintings on tombs that traditions of dancing date back to ancient Egyptian times. Today, *raqs sharqi*, or belly dancing, is performed only by women. Another popular dance, often performed at weddings, is for men only. It is called the *Tahteeb* dance. The men stand opposite each other and dance with thick, wooden sticks.

Festivals through the year

There are both Islamic and Christian festivals throughout the Egyptian year. The main **Muslim** festivals are Eid al-Fitr, which celebrates the end of Ramadan, Moulid an-Nabi celebrating the birth of the Prophet Muhammad, and Eid al-Adha, which marks the time of year when Muslims go on the *hajj* – a pilgrimage to the holy city of Makkah in Saudi Arabia. The most important time of year for Coptic Christians is Easter.

A stall selling delicious Egyptian food during the festival of Eid al-Fitr.

Nobel Prize prize awarded every year to people who have made great achievements in physics, chemistry, medicine, literature, and peace

The first Monday after the Coptic Easter is Sham al-Nessim, which means "smell of the breeze". This spring festival has its roots in ancient Egyptian history, and is a national holiday celebrated by all Egyptians. People go on outings and take picnics of traditional food, including salted fish, called *feseekh*, spring onions, and coloured eggs.

Moulids

Other festivals celebrate local saints. These festivals are called *moulids*, and they are held at different times all over the country. They are the places to hear traditional music, watch daring horse riders, and see snake charmers. Sufi dancers often perform at moulids. The purpose of their dance is to go into a trance, which takes them nearer to Allah. Their chanting, swaying, and whirling can sometimes last for many hours.

Naguib Mahfouz

The Egyptian writer Naguib Mahfouz was born in Cairo in 1911. His writing earned him the **Nobel Prize** for Literature in 1988. Many of his novels are set in Cairo, particularly in the narrow streets and alleyways of the Islamic part of the city.

Sufi dancers perform at a festival in Cairo.

St Katherine's Monastery

At the foot of Mount Sinai, St Katherine's Monastery was founded in AD 527. According to the Bible, Moses received the **Ten Commandments** on Mount Sinai, and the monastery is believed to be built on the spot where God spoke to Moses through the burning bush.

St Katherine's Monastery on Mount Sinai has long been a place of pilgrimage for Christians.

Tourist hot-spots

Back in the centre of Cairo, you visit the island of Gezira. A quick ride in a lift and you're at the top of Cairo Tower. The Tower rises 185 metres (607 feet) into the air. From the top you can see as far as the pyramids of Giza to the west of the city. As you sip your hot chocolate in the café at the top of the Tower, you notice that someone has left a leaflet on your table: "Tourist hot-spots".

Giza

Just outside Cairo, the Giza pyramids are guarded by the huge Sphinx, a stone statue of a creature with a human head and the body of a lion. Of the Seven Wonders of the Ancient World, the pyramids are the only ones you can still see today.

The mysterious Sphinx guards the tombs of the **pharaohs** at Giza.

WORD BANK New Kingdom period from 1550 to 1070 BC in ancient Egypt
Old Kingdom period from 2686 to 2181 BC in ancient Egypt

Saqqara

South of Cairo lies Saqqara, the royal burial place for the capital of the **Old Kingdom**, Memphis. There are eleven large pyramids – including the Pyramid of Djoser, one of the most famous sights in Egypt – and countless other tombs.

Luxor

Luxor grew out of the ruins of the capital of the **New Kingdom** of ancient Egypt, Thebes. There is so much to see, it's difficult to know where to start! Visit the huge temples at Luxor and Karnak on the east bank of the Nile. Then cross to the west bank to experience the breathtaking Hatsheput Temple and the Valley of the Kings, with its 62 royal tombs.

Hurghada

This resort on the Red Sea is one of the main centres for scuba diving. Here you can see the beautiful **coral** reefs along this stretch of coastline and go snorkelling to look at the colourful marine life (see page 42).

The famous Step Pyramid of Pharaoh Djoser at Saqqara. ▶

Ten Commandments ten laws given by God to Moses that form the basis of the Jewish and Christian religions

Stay or go?

You have travelled a long way from the far south of Egypt, through the desert to Cairo. You have seen some of the great monuments of ancient Egypt, experienced life in the desert, eaten Egyptian food, and been to an Egyptian soccer match. But there's so much more to do and see. So, should you go home or should you stay?

Preserving the reefs

Many tourists come to Egypt to dive around the beautiful **coral** reefs in the warm, clear waters of the Red Sea. But the reefs are very fragile, and it is easy to destroy them. Even touching the delicate coral can damage it. There are now laws to protect the reefs. At popular sites such as Hurghada, park rangers make sure that divers obey these laws.

Thousands of people visit the Red Sea every year to go scuba diving. The coral reef here is amazing.

WORD BANK fundamentalist person who follows religious laws and traditions very strictly

If you stayed in Egypt you could:

- Go windsurfing on Moon Beach on the Sinai Peninsula.
- Go to the Red Sea and do some snorkelling on the coral reefs.
- Take a ride in an air balloon across the desert.
- Visit the camel market at Birqash, north-west of Cairo.
- Explore the desert monasteries at **Wadi** Natrun.
- Go birdwatching at Lake Qarun.
- Get your hands and feet decorated with **henna**.

Henna is a kind of dye that Egyptian women use to paint beautiful patterns on their arms and hands, particularly for special occasions such as weddings.

Tourism threat

Egypt relies on tourism for a large part of its income. Since 1996, however, there have been several attacks on tourists by **Muslim fundamentalists**. After every attack, tourist numbers fall, causing great hardship to those Egyptians who rely on the tourist trade for their livelihoods.

43

Find out more

World Wide Web

If you want to find out more about Egypt you can search the Internet using keywords such as these:

- Egypt
- Cairo
- River Nile

You can also find your own keywords using headings or words from this book. Try using a search directory such as www.google.co.uk

Destination Detectives can find out more about Egypt by using the books and visiting the websites listed below:

The Egyptian Embassy

The Egyptian Embassy in your own country has lots of information about Egypt. You can find out about the different regions, the best times to visit, special events, and Egyptian culture. The embassy website address is: www.egypt.embassyhomepage.com

Further reading

100 Things You Should Know About Ancient Egypt, Jane Walker (Miles Kelly Publishing, 2004)

Countries of the World: Egypt, John Pallister (Evans, 2004)

Encyclopedia of Ancient Egypt (Usborne Publishing, 2004)

Eyewitness Guides: Ancient Egypt, George Hart (Dorling Kindersley, 2002)

Eyewitness Guides: Pyramid, James Putman, Peter Hayman, George Brightling (Dorling Kindersley, 2002)

Eyewitness Travel Guides: Egypt (Dorling Kindersley, 2003)

Visiting the Past: The Pyramids, Haydn Middleton (Heinemann Library, 2003)

Timeline

2650 BC
Pharaoh Djoser (Zoser) builds the Step Pyramid at Saqqara.

2589 BC
Pharaoh Khufu builds Great Pyramid at Giza.

2184 BC
Nitocris, the first female pharaoh, comes to power.

332 BC
Alexander the Great adds Egypt to his empire and founds Alexandria.

30 BC
Egypt becomes part of the Roman Empire.

AROUND AD 40
Christianity arrives in Egypt.

AD 394
Christianity becomes the official religion of Roman Egypt and all temples are closed down.

AD 640
Arab Muslim armies invade and conquer Egypt.

1798
Egypt is invaded by French armies, led by Napoleon Bonaparte.

1869
Opening of the Suez Canal.

1882
British troops occupy Egypt.

1922
Howard Carter discovers the tomb of Tutankhamun.

1948
First **Arab-Israeli War** as Egypt, Iraq, Jordan, and Syria attack the new state of Israel.

1953
Egypt becomes a republic.

1967
Israel takes control of the Sinai **Peninsula**.

1970
Completion of the Aswan High Dam.

1973
Egypt attacks Israel on Jewish holiday of Yom Kippur to reclaim Sinai Peninsula.

1979
Egypt signs Camp David peace agreement with Israel.

1982
Egypt regains control of the Sinai Peninsula from Israel.

2005
Presidential elections held in Egypt – president Mubarak is elected to his fifth term in office.

Egypt – facts & figures

The three colours, red, white, and black, were chosen to remind people of the struggle for independence from British rule. Red stands for bloodshed, white for revolution, and black for the end of the oppression of the Egyptian people. The bird in the centre of the flag is an eagle, the symbol of the great Muslim ruler Salah ad-Din.

Highs and lows
- Highest point: Mount Katherine (2,637 metres/8,652 feet)
- Lowest point: Qattara Depression in the Western Desert, which is 133 metres (436 feet) below sea level
- Only 2.87 percent of Egypt's total land area is used for farming
- 95 percent of Egypt's population live in the Nile Delta and Nile Valley.

People
- Population: 77.5 million
- Average life expectancy: 71 years
- Average number of children born per woman: 2.88
- Number of refugees living in Egypt: 70,215.

Technology
- Number of mobile phones: 8,583,940
- Number of cars: 23 per 1,000 people
- Number of doctors: 1 for every 459 people.

Glossary

AD time after Christ was born

afterlife life after death

ancestor person you are descended from

Arab person who originally came from the Arabian Peninsula

Arab-Israeli wars several wars fought between Israel and the Arab states in the 20th century

bazaar covered market full of stalls and small shops

BC Stands for "Before Christ"

cash crop crop that is grown for the farmer to sell

cemetery place where dead people are buried in graves or tombs

compressed natural gas gas from beneath the ground that has been squeezed into a container and can be used as a fuel

coral skeletons of tiny sea animals

delta area where a river splits into several channels as it flows into the sea

ethnic group people who share customs, beliefs, and often language

falcon bird of prey, often used for hunting

fava bean small bean that grows in pods

fertile land that is good for growing crops

flash flood violent flood that happens very quickly

floodplain area that floods when river water rises

fundamentalist person who follows religious laws and traditions very strictly

henna natural plant dye

hieroglyphics type of writing that uses pictures

hydroelectric energy created by moving water

irrigating using water from a river or reservoir to grow crops in fields

mechanized where machinery is used instead of human labour

mega-city huge urban area, often including several cities

metro rail system in an urban area

Middle Ages period of history from the 5th to the 15th centuries

minaret tall tower, usually built as part of a mosque

mosque place of worship for Muslims

muezzin man who gives the call to prayer to Muslims

Muslim person who belongs to the Islamic faith

New Kingdom period from 1550 to 1070 BC in ancient Egypt

Nobel Prize prize awarded every year to people who have made great achievements in physics, chemistry, medicine, literature, and peace

oasis fertile area in the middle of a desert

Old Kingdom period from 2686 to 2181 BC in ancient Egypt

peninsula narrow area of land that sticks out into the sea or a lake

pharaoh king or queen in ancient Egyptian times

porthole window in a boat

prehistoric time before written records began

rural relating to the countryside

Sahara largest desert in the world, covering much of North Africa

silt mud and sand

tahini paste made from sesame seeds

Ten Commandments ten laws given by God to Moses that form the basis of the Jewish and Christian religions

tram train that runs on rails set into the road and is powered by electricity

wadi dried-up river beds

Index

Titles in the *Destination Detectives* series include:

| Hardback | 1 406 20312 2 | Hardback | 1 406 20308 4 | Hardback | 1 406 20306 8 |

| Hardback | 1 406 20310 6 | Hardback | 1 406 20313 0 | Hardback | 1 406 20311 4 |

| Hardback | 1 406 20305 X | Hardback | 1 406 20307 6 | Hardback | 1 406 20314 9 |

Find out about the other titles in this series on our website www.raintreepublishers.co.uk